Identity Glitch

The Hidden Cost of Being Adaptable

Not Broken.
Not Behind.
Still Becoming.

Gretchen Lain, PhD

"Short. Honest. Human. No fixing. No pretending."

The most adaptable people are often the hardest to recognize - including to themselves.

I didn't write this to inspire you. I wrote this book so you wouldn't feel alone.

There are plenty of books about success, clarity, healing, and purpose.

There are fewer books about the middle...the long stretch of becoming where nothing is clean or conclusive.

This book is for the people who:

- Tried many paths
- Never felt exceptional
- Stayed anyway

If you see yourself in these pages, that isn't an accident. I wasn't trying to be unique. I was trying to be authentic. We are taught to tidy our stories. To extract lessons. To make meaning obvious. But most lives don't move that way. They move quietly. In patterns. In returns. With glitches, still processing.

If this book gives you language for something you couldn't name... That is enough. If it made you feel seen... That is surpassing the goal.

I don't know what my legacy will be. But I know this: I told the truth as carefully as I could. And I stayed.

TABLE OF CONTENTS

INTRODUCTION

- The Framework

DO YOU HAVE AN IDENTITY GLITCH?

- Self-Check

GLITCH I: BEGINNING YEARS

- Visibility & Survival

GLITCH II: PERFORMANCE

- Almost Good Enough

GLITCH III: QUESTIONING EVERYTHING

- Faith, Money, Identity

GLITCH IV: ADAPTATION

- Chameleon Mode

GLITCH V: ATTACHMENT

- Love & Learning

GLITCH VI: IDENTITY & WELLNESS

- Mental Noise, Neurodivergence & Misalignment

GLITCH VII: STILL BECOMING

- Not Broken. Not Behind. Still Becoming.

AFTERWORD

- Not Ending. Shifting Directions.

Framework Introduction

Framework

This book is built on a pattern most of us were never taught to see.

Every chapter follows four truths:

- The Experience - what happened to you
- The Survival Strategy - how to adapt
- The Misinterpretation - When the Survival Glitch Became Identity
- The Reframe - what was true all along

This framework exists for one reason: to separate your identity from your coping.

You are not your survival strategies or the conclusions you drew at twelve, eighteen, or thirty. You are not behind or broken.

You adapted. Once you understand what you are protecting, you can stop trying to adapt and instead find the next pathway.

It's time to stop surviving and start enjoying the journey of becoming!

Do You Have an Identity Glitch?

Do You Have an Identity Glitch?

The Identity Glitch Self-Check Directions.

Read each statement below and rate how often it feels true for you.

Use the scale:

0 - Not true for me

1 - Sometimes true

2 - Often true

Answer quickly. Your first instinct is usually the most accurate. Add up your score when you finish. This is not a clinical diagnosis. It is a reflection tool designed to help you notice patterns.

You may be experiencing the Identity Glitch if you:

- Adapt easily to different environments but struggle to define who you are
- Feel like you've lived many lives but none feel permanent
- Achieve things that look impressive externally but still feel "behind" internally
- Overanalyze yourself and constantly search for meaning
- Feel like your brain works differently from others
- Question career paths, beliefs, identity, or purpose more than the people around you

Interpreting Your Score

0-4 | Stable Identity Zone
You generally experience a clear sense of direction and identity. Occasional doubt is normal, but it does not dominate how you see yourself.

5-8 | Transitional Identity Zone
You may be moving through a period of change or questioning. Adaptation and exploration are part of your current development.

9-12 | Identity Glitch Pattern
You may have spent years adapting to different environments, expectations, and roles. This can create confusion between who you are and how you learned to survive.

The Identity Glitch does not mean you are broken or behind. It simply means your brain learned to adapt quickly.

This book will help you separate your identity from your coping strategies.

Glitch 1

Beginning years

Visibility & Survival

"What I am to be, I am now becoming"
~Benjamin Franklin.

The Experiences - What Happened

I was an unseen, homeschooled child. My classroom was the front seat of my parents' truck. I learned geography through motion and history through conversation.

In sixth grade, I entered public school. Suddenly, I was visible. Hallways were loud. Rules were spoken. Social hierarchies operated without instruction manuals. Everyone seemed to know something I didn't - how to be enough, how to evolve, and how to belong.

So I followed the intuition of my nervous system in an unfamiliar territory: observed, watched, and mirrored.

I wasn't awkward. I wasn't behind. I was gathering data. And data is how I learned to stay safe. I learned quickly that being noticed came with commentary. So survival meant adaptation.

I didn't realize it then, but the hidden cost of being adaptable was where my identity glitch began.

The Experiences - What Happened

Sixth grade not only came with the newness of school but it appeared... my body changed overnight too. The glitch... Massive breasts. Womanly figure. No warning.

Adults noticed before I understood why the new image mattered. Kids noticed before I knew how to respond.

For a moment, I was brave, visible, and a leader amongst my peers. I was proud of being in advanced classes, achieving high honors, belonging to the Future Problem Solvers of America state championship team, and being elected school president.

I believed I could change the world. Then the identity glitch occured... There were whispers, stares, and a cost for my image looking different.

Visibility stopped feeling empowering and started feeling like exposure. The body adapts first. Identity explains it later.

The Experience Reflection

(What happened to you)

When did your environment change faster than you were ready for?

When did you become visible before you felt prepared?

Where did your body, identity, or role shift before you had language for it?

What moments still feel sharp when you revisit them?

If you remove judgment, what actually happened?

The Survival Strategy - How to Adapt

For adaptable, highly-aware people, the survival strategies below are a system that becomes an identity system when in unfamiliar territory:

- Anticipate needs before they're spoken. Become who the environment rewards.
- Stay useful. Stay agreeable enough to stay safe. Shape-shift when necessary.
- Learn the rules fast - even the invisible ones. Perform competence. Study reactions. Minimize friction. Hide confusion.
- Earn belonging. Avoid becoming "too much." Scan for rejection before it arrives. Become easy to keep around.
- Make yourself valuable before authentic.
- Keep adjusting. Keep reading. Keep adapting.

It works. Until the realization sets in that you became fluent in everyone else... and unfamiliar to yourself.

The Survival Strategy - How to Adapt

When visibility becomes uncomfortable, don't soften, hunch, or disappear.

- Posture should never adapt to make others comfortable.
- Never apologize for taking up space.
- And when you question your enoughness... don't.
- Survival may have taught you camouflage.
- Peace will require visibility.
- Shape-shifting may earn acceptance, but it rarely brings peace.
- There is a difference between evolving and abandoning yourself.
- Do not let your armour become the knife in your side.

The Survival Strategy Reflection
(How you adapted)

How did you learn to read the room?

Where did you shrink, mirror, or overperform to stay safe?

What habits did you develop to avoid attention or earn approval?

What did you change about yourself to feel protected?

What strengths grew out of those adaptations?

The Misinterpretation -
When the Survival Glitch Became Identity

We misinterpret disinterest for awkwardness and misconceptions as being behind.

You are not a liability, risks are worth taking, and visibility remains, no matter how carefully you manage perception..

Stress is not the same as a lack of discipline.

It's okay to turn the extrovert on or the introvert off in the moments you need to.

You are the only being that can have total control of your thoughts, emotions, and actions.

Mirroring does not make you an imposter.

Don't confused adaptation with deficiency.

The Misinterpretation Reflection

(The story you told yourself)

What conclusions did you draw about who you were?

___

___

___

Where did you confuse adaptation with inadequacy?

___

___

___

What labels did you assign to yourself that may have been survival-based?

___

___

___

Where do you still believe you are "behind," "too much," or "not enough"?

___

___

___

What are you still punishing yourself for?

___

___

___

The Reframe -
What Was True All Along

It's not a glitch. It's an analitical processesing of the data. Reading the room is not insecurity - its methodical.

You are not behind, transitions are a piece of life.

At times, there is isolation; at others, immersion, neither come with a manual.

You adapted because your nervous system believed visibility carried risk. That was protection, not failure.

Leadership through observation is not timidity - it is strategic empathy.

Loss of focus on self is not laziness - its the fear of the pain that coinsides.

You're not disappearing, you're finding alternative survial routes.

You're not broken, it's okay to adapt when needed. Adaptation is not a flaw. It's evidence of forward movement.

The Reframe Reflection

(What was true all along)

What if your coping was intelligence, not weakness?

____

____

____

What if your body was protecting you?

____

____

____

What if reading the room was skill, not insecurity?

____

____

____

What if you weren't behind - just transitioning?

____

____

____

What would change if you separated who you are from how you survived?

____

____

____

Performance

Almost Good Enough

"Being good enough never is"

~Debbi Fields.

The Experience - What Happened

High school was rough.

The teasing didn't stop. It multiplied. So did the weight.

I searched for myself in the mirror and found someone I didn't recognize. What I saw felt like failure staring back. Shame made me smaller on the inside while my body took up more space.

At the same time, I was smart, I took accelerated college-prep. courses, multiple languages, and was consistently on the honor roll.

I sang in advanced choir - one of 300 to sing in Carnegie Hall. I stood on a stage in New York City, proud, holding a dozen roses. I didn't know how rare that was. I didn't let myself keep it. I felt defeated because sometimes I was a soprano and sometimes an alto. I learned how to harmonize without ever feeling like I belonged in the song.

The Experience - What Happened

Athletics told a similar story.

While I was part of numerous State finals teams, I was the one....

Falling over hurdles.

Warming the basketball bench.

Being cut from volleyball.

Not competitively cheering all three rounds.

I wasn't bad. But I wasn't enough.

Which meant I wasn't chosen.

And in high school, not being chosen feels like a lifelong sentence.

The Experience Reflection
(What happened to you)

Where in your life were you "almost" something - but not fully chosen?

When did achievement and insecurity exist at the same time?

Where were you performing well on paper but struggling internally?

What external successes did you minimize or dismiss?

What moments still feel like quiet disappointments you never named?

The Survival Strategy - How to Adapt

Do not shrink, physically or emotionally. Use your voice, be visible, believe in your certainty to be present in the moment.

Clap for others while swallowing disappointment. Contribute without the need for applause.

Actively learn the plays, show up, take integrity in yourself even when no one knows you are there.

Do not let shame echo louder than your dignity. Do not reach for coping mechanism. Put your gloves on and get in the ring.

Hold yourself accountable and take responsibility, then there are no fingers to point. Grow. Take risks. Stay. Go. Fail. Try again.

Consistency and resilience become armor.

The Survival Strategy Reflection
(How you adapted)

How did you cope when you felt not quite good enough?

___

___

___

Where did you shrink emotionally to avoid further disappointment?

___

___

___

What habits did you form to numb shame or pressure?

___

___

___

Where did consistency become your protection?

___

___

___

What did "showing up anyway" cost you - and what did it build in you?

___

___

___

The Misinterpretation - When the Survival Glitch Became Identity

Your not lazy, your busy, and that's not rationale enough to let your health take a back seat.

'Almost good enough" is average, sometimes seems Invisible, potentially replaceable. All of which are okay. You are exactly where you need to be at this moment.

Do not mistake resilience for mediocrity and endurance for insignificance. Take the opportunity to shine in one lane, with half a headlight or two high beams. Your talents are unique to you.

You don't lacked discipline, you lack a reason to keep going. You don't lack confident, you aren't valuing your true worth.

Don't confuse safety with stagnation, protection with weakness, and persistence with failure. These are all a part of being here, in this very moment.

The Misinterpretation Reflection

(The story you told yourself)

Where did you label yourself as lazy, average, or undisciplined?

What did "almost good enough" teach you to believe about your worth?

Where do you still assume you are replaceable?

Did you mistake resilience for mediocrity?

What strengths have you dismissed because they weren't flashy?

The Reframe - What Was True All Along

Overwhelmed can look like lazy.

Shame can posture as a lack of discipline.

Grief will form the minute you turn your head.

"Almost good enough" is not a verdict; It is evidence that of resilience.

Resilience rarely looks glamorous; Persistence rarely looks impressive, but it lasts.

Even bench warmers can continue to build skill, endurance, consistency, and depth.

Your not stuck. Your spinning.

Your not behind; your building capacity.

And mediocrity...often ends up being durability.

The Reframe Reflection

(What was true all along)

What if persistence is more powerful than brilliance?

What if durability matters more than dominance?

Where have you built depth quietly?

What if being "almost chosen" meant you were still developing capacity?

What would shift if you saw consistency as strength instead of stagnation?

Glitch III

Questioning Everything

Faith, Money, Identity

"Question everything.
Learn something.
Answer nothing"
~Euripides.

The Experience - What Happened

In my early twenties, I gave health a second chance. Not to get thin, but to understand health. This time, it wasn't about shame. It was about curiosity. I hired a trainer, not to punish my body, but to learn how it worked.

I relearned nutrition and unlearned that health didn't come from perfection or discipline; it came from resiliency. I no longer wanted to be at war with myself, my reflection. Movement became something I practiced, and sweat meant effort.

It wasn't perfect. It wasn't consistent. But I kept showing up.

For the first time, health felt like a healthy relationship, one that would require work but was worth the effort.

This tribute didn't erase the past; it wasn't a quick fix, it was to see what might be possible.

I am not my shape. I am the person inside it.

The Experience - What Happened

At the same time, I began questioning everything.My thinking wasn't linear. My thoughts looped. My words came sideways. I struggled with recall, with memory, with focus. ADHD. Dyslexia. Hyperfocus. An average IQ score that felt like a quiet indictment.

I was raised Christian. I believed answers existed. Then I grew questions I couldn't un-ask. I didn't know what was true. I did know what felt honest. Some days, faith looked like belief. Some days, it looks like staying open. Both counted, I am allowed to not know and still be okay.

My father died. Grief rearranged everything - faith, focus, nervous system. Loss didn't end belief. It complicated it. Questions resurfaced about religion and the afterlife. Death touched my focus, relationships, and nervous system. Loss doesn't end. It changes shape. It brings more questions.

The Experience - What Happened

I grew up with little - not just little money, but even the language about money. Scarcity was normal. Planning was survival. When I finally had income, I spent it. Not recklessly - symbolically.

Spending felt like freedom. Saving felt like fear. I didn't know how to hold money because I had never seen it modeled. Hand-me-down expectations. I learned to stretch and adapt. To never assume abundance.

Scarcity stayed longer than it needed to. I was well into my 40s before I overcame the "I don't deserve, less than, poor mindset and image" that I held onto like a survival badge of honor.

I still want things. But I learned to pause. Because stuff isn't as important as experiences, memories, and togetherness.

Saving isn't deprivation anymore. Its direction. Choosing the future-together-feels better than anything I ever bought.

The Experience - What Happened

I was a middle child - flexible, adaptable, sometimes invisible. I wanted to speak, but waited to be invited.

I studied other women to understand what "pretty" meant. Dressed older to feel safer. Covered to feel controlled. Clothes weren't expression - they were protection. I wasn't choosing style; I was choosing safety. How to be seen without performing. It's about asking: Can I see myself today without judgment? Some days the answer is yes. Some days I'm still working on it. Both are allowed.

I was ordinary... and that was enough. That used to hurt. Now it feels grounded. The reality is, most people aren't extraordinary.

I was learning the difference between kindness and self-erasure. I learned that being agreeable kept the peace. I softened myself so others wouldn't leave. I didn't realize until later in life that kindness without boundaries becomes self-erasure.

The Experience Reflection

(What happened to you)

What areas of your life have shifted from certainty to questioning?

Where did grief change your beliefs?

What messages about money did you inherit without realizing?

When did you begin doubting your intelligence or capability?

Where did you learn to hide rather than express?

The Survival Strategy - How to Adapt

Optimize.

Make your health part of the structure. Analyze faith. Don't make money into a symbol of worth.

Softened when you need peace. Agree to avoid contention. Studied social cues to find your medium.

When your brain feels nonlinear, take notice and compensate.

When you feel ordinary, aim higher.

Adaptation is a language; neither good nor bad if it's controlled

The Survival Strategy Reflection
(How you adapted)

How do you try to regain control when life feels uncertain?

Where did you become agreeable to stay connected?

What did you spend money on to prove something to yourself?

Where did you overcompensate for perceived cognitive weaknesses?

How did you protect yourself socially or spiritually?

The Misinterpretation -
When the Survival Glitch Became Identity

Be curious. Ask questions, this is not weakness, you are a truth seeker.

Scarcity does not have to be your identity.

Nnonlinear thinking doesn't mean you aren't smart and average doesn't make you invisible. Ordinary can be beyond remarkable.

Don't confuse curiosity with instability.

Don't confuse adaptability with a lack of identity.

Don't confuse cognitive differences with intellectual deficiency.

The Misinterpretation Reflection

(The story you told yourself)

What labels did you assign to yourself that were rooted in fear?

___

___

___

Where did you mistake questioning for failing?

___

___

___

How has scarcity shaped your self-image?

___

___

___

What cognitive differences have you misinterpreted as flaws?

___

___

___

Where do you still equate "ordinary" with "not enough"?

___

___

___

The Reframe -
What Was True All Along

Health is a life sentence, and you only get one chance to get it right. Reconcile with yourself and find a medium.

Questions aren't rebellion. They are integrity.

Scarcity thinking wasn't identity. It is often an inheritance.

Nonlinear thought isn't a lack of intelligence. It is system processing thought patterns; it's wiring, and it varies per person. It's not incompetence. It a processing variable.

Ordinary isn't a verdict. It's reality. And most people live there ... in the middle.

It's an evolving. Build discernment, intelligence., and except your hard drive because they are each wired a little bit differently. And differen is not a deficient.

The Reframe Reflection

(What was true all along)

What if your questions are a sign of depth, not doubt?

What if your money habits were inherited, not character flaws?

What if your brain works differently - and that's an asset?

What if "ordinary" is freedom from performance?

What if you are not confused - just becoming more honest?

Adaptation

Chameleon Mode

"It is not the strongest of the species that survives, nor the most intelligent that survives. It is the one that is the most adaptable to change"

~Charles Darwin.

The Experience - What Happened

For most of my life, I adapted before I understood who I was. I became a boundaryless chameleon. "No" felt like rejection, like danger; so I said yes and paid for it later...

Different environments required different versions of me. So I became them. Employee. Friend. Partner. Leader.

Each room had its own expectations, its own social language, its own definition of competence.

I learned to read those expectations quickly and adjust.

From the outside, it looked like flexibility. From the inside, it felt like fragmentation, erasure.

Sometimes I forgot what was real and became determined to learn to stop blending in long enough to be seen and heard.

I am tired of proving. I don't want to justify my existence. I want to inhabit it.

The Experience - What Happened

I struggled with memory and recall. Instructions sometimes slipped through my mind like water through open hands.

I get bored easily. Repetition drains me. Novelty wakes me up. Interest fuels focus more than discipline ever could. I am capable of deep focus.

When something clicks, I disappear into it. Time bends. Ideas multiply. This isn't inconsistency; it's intensity without scaffolding.

My thoughts didn't move in straight lines - they looped, jumped, connected sideways. ADHD. Dyslexia. Hyperfocus. I didn't understand those words yet. All I knew was that my brain worked differently. Tests told me I had an average IQ. I interpreted that as confirmation that I wasn't especially intelligent.

I didn't yet understand that intelligence comes in many forms - and that pattern recognition, systems thinking, and human insight rarely show up on standardized tests. I finally saw myself in the research.. I wasn't failing life. I was just misaligned.

The Experience - What Happened

I am a fixer. If I could fix it, I could control it. thought an education or a career would give me value. I didn't know that worth isn't issued with a degree or by a title. My career became an experiment. Retail manager. Sales. Merchandiser. Golf course assistant. Kitchen prep chef. Nanny. Housekeeper.

Later, more formal roles followed. HR. Children's services investigator. Foster home pseudo-attorney. Research scientist. Industrial-organizational psychologist. IT systems development. Professional coaching. Leadership.

Each job taught me something. None felt like home.

I thought prestige would settle me; It didn't. It sharpened the question instead.

I am a square peg trying to fit into a round hole.

I have done many things. None feel permanent. Maybe permanence was the wrong goal.

WORTH... maybe that's where I should be looking.

The Experience - What Happened

I moved through Fortune 100 companies and prestigious institutions. Impressive logos. Smart rooms. Fast minds.

From the outside, it looked like an arrival. From the inside, it felt like a performance. I kept up. I delivered results. People trusted my work.

But a quiet question followed me everywhere: Do I actually belong here?

I entered the intelligence community, carrying responsibilities that came with quiet pressure and heavy stakes. I learned how secrecy feels in the body - how responsibility can sit in your nervous system long after the workday ends.

The Experience - What Happened

Identifying health must come first; my body began to protest.

Chronic back pain forced a truth I had been avoiding: this body was the only one I had.

Health stopped being optional.

For the first time, taking care of myself wasn't about appearance or approval; it wasn't punishment, it was about preservation.

I made a cognitive choice, not to be thin, but not to be wheelchair bound, which meant I needed to be at a minimum, functional. And that was enough to begin a full revamp of life dedicated to my health.

That choice became the first act of self-respect, self-love, and continued self-care.

The Experience Reflection
(What happened to you)

Where in your life have you adapted to multiple environments?

___

___

___

What roles have you taken on to meet the expectations around you?

___

___

___

When did your work look successful on the outside but uncertain on the inside?

___

___

___

What signals has your body given you when something in your life was unsustainable?

___

___

___

Where have you been searching for belonging through achievement?

___

___

___

The Survival Strategy - How to Adapt

Adaptation sometimes becomes a primary skill.

It's easier to lbecome what the room needs.
It is simple to adapt, deliver what is required from the environment versus going against the grain.

All too often if the environment request, us adaptable people deliver.

But this flexibility comes with a cost.

When you continuously say yes when you should have said no, ..."No" feels dangerous - like rejection, like abandonment, like failure.

So we adapt, flex, and stretch until we are fully overextended myself.

We work harder, and Give more.

.

Approval felel safer than authenticity!

Being useful becomes the way we measure value if we dont learnto say no..

The Survival Strategy - How to Adapt

Repetition drains. Curiosity fuels.

Focus comes with interest. Time disappeared,. Ideas multiplied.

Without meaning, motivation evaporates.

Adadaptible people are often, "fixers." We fix, solve, and solution to avoid self uncertainty.

Helping others survive broken systems becomes part of the adaptable identity.

Underneath it all there is a quieter question...:f I stop adapting,, who am I?

The Survival Strategy Reflection

(How you adapted)

How have you adapted to meet the expectations of different environments?

Where do you say yes when your body wants to say no?

When do you over-give in order to feel valuable?

What types of work activate your focus and curiosity?

Where have you taken responsibility for fixing problems that were never yours to carry?

The Misinterpretation -
When the Survival Glitch Became Identity

Adaptability doesn't meant we lac identity.

Fitting and belongingare not synonymous. .

Istop saying you're inconsistent and scattered..

There is no roadmap of life, a singular path we are meant to follow, we are allowed to have free will.

IIt's patchwork, and that's okay.

Jobs. Unterests. Directions. Trials. Errors. Failure. Successes.

We adapt to grow.

The Misinterpretation -
When the Survival Glitch Became Identity

Reecall or focus, doesnt equate to intelligence..

Career changes don't make you unstable, they make you unstoppable.

There is nothing wrong with uestioning your purpose, it keeps us aware of reality.

We work hard for achievements and recognition but instant gratification fleets quickly.

Degrees. Credentials. Prestige. They look impressive but dont usually fill the void.

Permanence can be the goal but doesn't have to be.

Certainty can be the destination, but you can continue on if, there doesn't have to be a final stop.

The Misinterpretation Reflection
(The story you told yourself)

Where have you labeled yourself as inconsistent or scattered?

What beliefs have you formed about success based on traditional career paths?

How have you interpreted cognitive differences as personal shortcomings?

Where do you feel pressure to justify your existence through achievement?

What parts of your story have you mistaken for failure?

The Reframe - What Was True All Along

You're not directionless. you are still taking in the views.

Every experience is data.

Every job is a classroom.

Every system worked teaches us something about how humans function - motivation, power, leadership, failure.

Nonlinear thinking isn't a weakness. It was pattern recognition.

Adaptability isnt identity loss. It is environmental intelligence.

Career shifts aren't instability. They are exploration.

The Reframe -
What Was True All Along

Credentials dont make us special., they give us technical language.

The language for behaviors, systems, and patterns

You are not failing life. Misalignment happens.

Environments don't work. We dont fit. The wiring was off somewhere and it was causing a glitch...And thats okay.

Stop limiting yourself to a single lane. Recognize the breadth. Of the drive.

You are not behind.. Life is a journey, not a destination.

IBuildi a wide lens because wide lenses capture more of the light, beauty, and scenery.

Enjoy the once in a lifetime view.

The Reframe Reflection

(What was true all along)

What if your career shifts were exploration instead of failure?

What if your adaptability is a form of intelligence?

Where have you gathered more experience than you realized?

What patterns do you see across the roles you've held?

What if you are not directionless - just multidimensional?

Glitch V

Failure

Failures & Comebacks

"The phoenix must burn to emerge"

~Janet Fitch.

The Experience - What Happened

My early understanding of love was built on trust without instruction.

I trusted easily. I assumed people meant what they said. I believed good intentions were enough to keep relationships safe.

No one had ever explained consent to me.

No one had modeled boundaries in a way I could recognize.

I didn't yet know that desire could exist without obligation, or that attention could exist without ownership.

When romantic attention arrived, I interpreted it as value.

The Experience - What Happened

Some of the sexual situations I entered were not violent or dramatic. They were quiet, confusing, and hard to name.

I said yes when my body said no because I believed that was what kindness required.

When something felt wrong, I assumed the fault belonged to me.

Shame followed quickly. I blamed my body. My face. My reflection.

I believed desire was something I owed in exchange for acceptance.

That belief stayed with me longer than the relationships themselves.

The Experience - What Happened

At eighteen, I married.

I believed love could conquer anything if I just tried hard enough.

Commitment meant endurance. Sacrifice meant loyalty.

I worked at the relationship with the same persistence I had applied everywhere else in my life.

But love does not heal addiction by willpower alone.

Substance abuse overtook the marriage.

I became codependent, trying to fix a situation that was never mine to repair.

The Experience - What Happened

I believed if I loved harder, stayed longer, sacrificed more, the relationship would stabilize.

It didn't.

Eventually the marriage ended.

The divorce felt like public failure.

I had entered marriage believing it was permanent, believing that walking away meant weakness.

But staying had begun to cost me my safety, my dignity, and my sense of self.

Leaving wasn't giving up. It was survival.

The Experience - What Happened

I entered another relationship. I became engaged again, and I hoped the lessons of the past had prepared me.

At first it felt safer.

But quiet warning signs began to surface: controlling dynamics, emotional manipulation, and conflict that required me to shrink instead of speaking up.

Hope became louder than truth.

For a while, I ignored the signals.

Then I realized that love requiring fear is not love.

Walking away hurt deeply, but it hurt less than staying.

The Experience - What Happened

Two failed relationships

I began to question everything.

Was I bad at love?

Was something wrong with me?

Why did I keep choosing the same dynamics?

For the first time.

I stopped asking how to fix the relationship.

And began asking how to understand the pattern.

The Experience Reflection

(What happened to you)

Where did you first learn what love was supposed to look like?

____

____

____

What relationships shaped your early beliefs about consent, safety, and commitment?

____

____

____

When did you stay longer than your instincts wanted you to?

____

____

____

What experiences still carry shame that may not belong to you?

____

____

____

Where did walking away feel like failure even when it protected you?

____

____

____

The Survival Strategy - How to Adapt

The survival strategy in relationships is endurance.

If something felt unstable, work harder.

If conflict emerges, it's either flight or fight. Determine if you need to soften or stand your ground.

If there is a struggle, realize you don't always have to find or become the solution.

Don't confused love with labor.

Helping shouldn't be your language for intimacy.

The Survival Strategy - How to Adapt

Patience doesn't mean loyalty.

Sacrifice doesn't mean commitment.

The strongest relationships are not the ones that survive the most difficulty.

Adapt with love not for love.

Don't adapt to be agreeable. Don't adapt to be accommodating. Don't take responsibililty for emotional climates that were never your to regulate.

When boundaries feel uncomfortable, don't avoid them, test them.

"No" shouldn't feel dangerous.

"No" shouldn't mean rejection.

"No" shouldn't mean abandonment.

"No" shouldn't mean conflict.

The Survival Strategy - How to Adapt

Don't always say, "yes".

Don't say, yes to conversations you aren't ready for.

Don't say, yes to expectations you don't agree with.

Don't say, yes to emotional burdens you could not carry alone.

The yes strategy only works for a short while. It kept relationships intact. It kept people close.... temporarily, and it came with a cost.

Exhaustion.

Resentment.

Confusion.

Eventually, you will realize... endurance is not the same thing as love.

The Survival Strategy Reflection
(How you adapted)

How have you tried to maintain relationships by working harder instead of setting boundaries?

Where do you take responsibility for other people's behavior or emotions?

When does patience turn into self-abandonment?

What fears arise when you consider saying "no"?

What patterns of endurance have shaped your relationships?

The Misinterpretation - When the Survival Glitch Became Identity

We often tell ourselves... we are the problem.

Failed relationships, must be something we did wrong.

We assume we lack the judgment, intuition, and ability to choose wisely.

We think other people are better at relationships than we are.

When conflict appears, we interpreted it as evidence that we need to improve.

We believe more patient, more understanding, more forgiving, and the relationship will stabilize.

We mistake familiarity for fate and endurance for strength.

We believe love required suffering and leaving means weakness.

The Misinterpretation - When the Survival Glitch Became Identity

We carry shame about experiences when moments are confusing.

We struggle to name experiences in a positive way with a growers mentality.

Without proper language, we assume responsibility.

We question our ability to know rights from from wrongs.

Sometimes we relive and deepen the wounds of experiences without forgiving ourselves and growing more aware of what we need.

Understanding, forgiveness, and knowledge come with time.

Boundaries must be learned before they can be enforced.

The Misinterpretation Reflection

(The story you told yourself)

What conclusions have you drawn about yourself because of past relationships?

____

____

____

Where have you confused endurance with emotional strength?

____

____

____

What experiences have you blamed yourself for without context?

____

____

____

When have you mistaken familiar dynamics for healthy ones?

____

____

____

What beliefs about love might actually be inherited misunderstandings?

____

____

____

The Reframe -
What Was True All Along

You are not bad at love. There are always lessons to be learned.

You have to define the boundaries of yourself, your body, your love.

Find a healthy relationship, understand their boundaries, create a list of must have's, won't allow, and make that list your ancor in the sand.

You can't practice a skill you had never been used.

Past relationships are not evidence of failure.

They are evidence of experiences. Each an opportunity to learn and clarified what you want.

Learn the difference between...

Attention and respect.

Patience and self-erasure.

Commitment and captivity.

The Reframe - What Was True All Along

Eventually, you will return to the relationship class - but this time with a different intention.

Not to impress.

To understand.

Strengthened your emotional intelligence.

Learn to communicate more clearly.

Established boundaries that protect both people in the relationship.

And stop thinking that love required self-abandonment.

The Reframe - What Was True All Along

Build the next relationship slowly, deliberately, and with awareness.

It will not be perfect, but ground it in mutual support, respect, and friendship.

Love, is not the absence of difficulty. It is the presence of safety.

One day you will look back and instead of seeing failed relationships... you will see evidence that you chose honesty over comfort.

With every ended relationship is the opportunity to grow.

Those chapters do not define your being. They reveal courage.

You are not broken. You are learning, and growth requires trying again.

The Reframe Reflection

(What was true all along)

What if your past relationships were classrooms rather than verdicts?

What have you learned about love that you didn't know before?

How do healthy boundaries change the meaning of commitment?

What patterns have you interrupted that once felt inevitable?

What does safer love look like for you today?

Glitch VI

Wellness

Mental Noise, Neurodivergence, & Misalignment

"Our wounds are often the openings into the best and most beautiful part of us"

~David Richo.

My Experience - What Happened

My mind has always been loud.

Not loud in the way people expect anxiety to look. Not dramatic. Not visibly unraveling.

Functional. The kind that smiles, over-prepares, and quietly runs every possible outcome in the background.

Negative self-talk. What-ifs. Replays.

My brain becomes busiest when the world goes quiet.

Sometimes the noise is anxiety. Sometimes it's sadness.

Not constant depression, but periods where the weight settles in and makes everything slower.

Enough to notice. Enough to make me aware.

My Experience - What Happened

I have also always lived with a strange contradiction.

I love people. Connection energizes me. And yet people drain me.

I am an extrovert who needs the recovery time of an introvert.

For years I interpreted that exhaustion as weakness. I assumed something must be wrong with me because social energy didn't function the way it seemed to for others.

My thoughts rarely move in straight lines. They jump between ideas, loop back, and connect concepts in ways that sometimes surprise even me.

My Experience - What Happened

My memory doesn't always cooperate.

I forget things I genuinely care about.

I lose track of instructions in long conversations.

I sometimes nod along in meetings while silently panicking because my brain is still trying to sort what was said two sentences ago.

This doesn't mean I'm unintelligent.

But for many years, it made me feel that way.

Tests often placed me in the middle.

Average IQ. Average personality scores. Average aptitude markers.

Nothing exceptional. Nothing deficient.

Just... mid-range. I interpreted that as invisibility.

My Experience - What Happened

Meanwhile, my mind was producing ideas faster than my systems could hold them.

I could see patterns easily. I could see where organizations, teams, and strategies should go.

Vision came naturally. Execution was harder.

Momentum often disappeared when structure was missing.

Tasks stalled not because of lack of care, but because my brain needed scaffolding it didn't yet know how to build.

For a long time I assumed these differences meant I was flawed.

It would take years before I learned a different explanation.

The Experience Reflection

(What happened to you)

What patterns do you notice in your internal dialogue?

When does your mind feel loudest or hardest to quiet?

In what situations do you feel energized by people, and when do you feel drained?

What experiences have made you question your intelligence or capability?

When have you felt misunderstood because your brain processes information differently?

The Survival Strategy - How to Adapt

To manage the noise in the mind, you must develop strategies.

Some will be helpful. Some will be exhausting.

Preparation becomes armor.

If you anticipat every possible outcome, you could prevent mistakes. If you plan, rehearse, and study enough, maybe the chaos in your mind would stay contained.

Over-preparing helps appear composed. When inside, it's often constant cognitive traffic.

When memory failed, it's easy to compensate with effort, work harder, and double-check details.

It's easy to build plans that help others succeed, even when your own systems struggle to keep pace.

The neaurodivergent brain learns to rely on intensity.

The Survival Strategy - How to Adapt

When something captures interest, does the focus shift for you? Do hours pass unnoticed? Ideas multiplied rapidly?

Can you effortlessly align teams, create systems, and inspire momentum.

When something lacks meaning, does your motivation evaporate. Often we interpret this fluctuation as inconsistency.

In reality, it is just an alternative neurological wiring.

The brain needs stimulation, structure, and clarity. Without those conditions, the system stalls. There's a glitch.

Socially, we learn to adapt by masking confusion.

If conversations moved too quickly, lines get blurred neurodivergents wait for context clues later.

This is how we adapt to the glitch.

The Survival Strategy - How to Adapt

We try to appear capable even when the internal processing "blue wheel of death" is still spinning and loading.

It's okay to push through, until we are over-exhaused.

Don't make promises unless you fully intend to follow through, find a system to do so.

We don't forget to follow through because we don't care - it's because memory isn't governed by willpower alone, and strategy to support our shortcomings is a must.

Be persistence...

Even when your brain feels scattered.

Even when your systems break down.

Even when the effort required to function feels disproportionate.

There will be a system reboot on the other side.

The Survival Strategy Reflection
(How you adapted)

How do you compensate when your mind feels overwhelmed or distracted?

Where do you over-prepare to manage uncertainty?

When do you rely on intensity or bursts of focus to complete work?

How do you mask confusion or overload in conversations or meetings?

What habits have helped you function even when your internal experience feels chaotic?

The Misinterpretation - When the Survival Glitch Became Identity

We often believe our brain is defective.

When tasks are forgotten, we call ourselves careless.

When attention wanders, we call ourselves lazy.

When we struggle to articulate thoughts quickly in conversation, we call ourselves unintelligent.

Every missed detail becomes evidence that we are failing. Every forgotten task reinforces the belief that we lacked discipline.

We interprete mishaps as confirmation that we are ordinary or not enough.

We let our "average" become invisible. We let our "invisible" became unimportant. We let our "unimportant" become a never ending glitch in the system of our mind.

The Misinterpretation - When the Survival Glitch Became Identity

We misunderstand anxiety.

Instead of seeing it as a nervous system trying to manage uncertainty, we treat it like a personal weakness, a failpoint, an error in the system.

The same is true for depression.

We believed those heavy moments meant something was wrong with our character, instead of recognizing them as signals from a system under strain.

Most damaging of all, we believe the noise in the mind measn instability.

That belief shapes the way we see ourselves.

Until we allow new language to enter into our lives.

The Misinterpretation Reflection

(The story you told yourself)

What labels have you assigned to yourself when your mind doesn't function the way you expect?

When have you mistaken neurological differences for character flaws?

Where have you interpreted "average" as meaning invisible or insignificant?

How has anxiety shaped the way you evaluate yourself?

What stories about your mind might need revisiting?

The Reframe -
What Was True All Along

The truth is simpler than the story we tell ourselves.

.

It's okay for our brains to work differently.

It's not incorrectly, it's just differet.

Being neurodivergent doesn't suddenly appear later in life. It is present, we simply lack the coding language to recognize it.

What we often call distraction is actually pattern scanning.

What we refer to as inconsistency is usually intensity searching for structure.

What we sometimes label as forgetfulness is generally a brain that requires external anchors.

Thinking is systemic. It's okay to see patterns before details, direction before steps, and possibilities before processes.

The Reframe -
What Was True All Along

That kind of cognition can struggle in environments designed for linear thinkers.

But it also creates insight.

The same mind that forgets small tasks can build complex strategies.

The same brain that struggles with recall can recognize patterns across systems and people.

And the same people who once believed they were invisible now understand something important...

Most lives exist in the middle.

Not extraordinary.

Not deficient.

Just human.

The Reframe -
What Was True All Along

Having a mid-range system does not mean you are insignificant.

It means being part of the majority of humanity quietly navigating complexity.

We are all, still learning how our brain works.

We are all still building systems to support it.

And the truths is now more clearer than ever...

You are not lazy, careless, or unintelligent.

You are wired differently, and that's okay.

Different doesn't mean....

Broken or behind....

It means your still becoming.

The Reframe Reflection

(What was true all along)

What if your brain works differently rather than incorrectly?

Where might your cognitive style actually be an advantage?

What systems could help support the way your mind naturally operates?

How would your self-talk change if you viewed neurological differences with curiosity instead of judgment?

What parts of your mind deserve compassion rather than criticism?

Glitch VII

My Still Becoming Message To You!

Not Broken. Not Behind. Still Becoming.

"At fifty-four, I am still in progress, and I hope that I always will be"

~Michelle Obama.

The Experience - What Happened

By some definitions, I am not successful.
I am an author without a bestseller.

An entrepreneur still searching for traction.

A thinker with more ideas than finished systems.

For a long time, I measured myself harshly against metrics that were never designed for lives like mine.

Productivity.

Recognition.

Certainty.

Those seemed to be the measures that mattered. But life is not lived in clean milestones. It unfolds in quieter ways.

Some days, my life feels full.

Other days, it feels unfinished.

The Experience - What Happened

I am a daughter, sister, wife, friend, aunt, dog mom, colleague.

I manage a household. I grow food in the garden. I grocery shop, meal prep, cook, clean, organize schedules, host gatherings, plan events, manage finances, coordinate contractors, and maintain a thousand small details that make daily life possible.

I write books. I build businesses.

I design my own websites and develop my own ideas.

And still, some days I feel behind. Not because I am doing nothing.

Because the work of living is invisible.

The Experience - What Happened

There is also another layer beneath the busyness.

A nervous system that remains cautious.

I scan rooms for tone shifts. I notice energy changes quickly. I am suspicious of safety, not because I want to be, but because my life taught me vigilance before it taught me ease.

Trust feels expensive.

So I ration it.

At times, I am tired in ways that sleep cannot fix.

The kind of tired that comes from holding responsibility in many directions at once.

And yet, even in that exhaustion, I continue showing up.

Not heroically. Honestly.

Still here. Still trying.

The Experience Reflection

(What happened to you)

What invisible labor fills your days?

How do you currently measure success in your life?

Where do you still feel behind even when you are working hard?

What responsibilities quietly shape your daily energy?

When do you notice yourself scanning for threat instead of experiencing ease?

The Survival Strategy - How I Adapted

For most of my life, survival mode guided my decisions.

It helped me stay alert. It helped me navigate unpredictable situations. It helped me adapt quickly when circumstances changed.

Survival mode can be incredibly effective.

It sharpens attention. It motivates action. It pushes people forward even when conditions are difficult.

But survival mode also comes with a cost.

When your nervous system learns vigilance first, rest can feel unfamiliar.

Safety can feel suspicious.

You continue preparing for problems long after the danger has passed.

The Survival Strategy - How I Adapted

I developed strategies to function inside that tension.
I worked harder. I became responsible.

I learned emotional intelligence not as a philosophical concept, but as a survival skill.

Naming emotions helped me regulate them.
Understanding other people's motivations helped me navigate conflict.

I also learned to keep going even when discouraged.
Even when the projects moved slowly.

Even when recognition didn't come.

Even when my efforts looked small from the outside.

Persistence became my strategy.

If I kept showing up, maybe things would eventually make sense.

The Survival Strategy Reflection
(How you adapted)

What survival habits helped you navigate difficult seasons of life?

Where do you continue operating in survival mode even when circumstances have changed?

What strategies have helped you manage emotional stress or uncertainty?

How does persistence show up in your life?

When do you push through exhaustion instead of pausing?

The Misinterpretation - When the Survival Glitch Became my Identity

For many years, I misunderstood my own life.

I believed unfinished work meant failure.

I believed uncertainty meant weakness.

I believed being tired meant I lacked discipline.

I believed being cautious meant I lacked trust.

I believed that if my work did not produce visible success quickly, it meant I was falling behind.

The harshest misunderstanding was the way I interpreted my past.

I asked the wrong question. What's wrong with me?

Why do I struggle in areas that seem easy for others?

Why haven't I arrived yet? That question kept me stuck.

The Misinterpretation -
When the Survival Glitch Became my Identity

Because it assumes the problem is the person.

It assumes something inside is broken.

But much of what I experienced was not failure.
It was misalignment.

Misalignment between environments and wiring.

Misalignment between expectations and reality.

Misalignment between survival habits and present circumstances.

Once I began to see that distinction, something important shifted.

The Misinterpretation Reflection

(The story you told yourself)

What harsh conclusions have you drawn about your life or abilities?

____

____

____

Where have you mistaken slow progress for failure?

____

____

____

What beliefs about success might need reevaluating?

____

____

____

How has survival thinking shaped your expectations of yourself?

____

____

____

What questions about your life might be keeping you stuck?

____

____

____

The Reframe - What Was True All Along

None of the glitches in my life meant I was broken.

They meant I was learning. They meant I was adapting. They meant I was becoming.

The most important shift happened when I changed the question.

Instead of asking: What's wrong with me? I began asking: What do I need?

What systems support the way my mind works? What relationships support the way my heart works? What environments support the way I contribute best?

Those questions changed everything. Not instantly. Not perfectly. But steadily.

The work of becoming is not dramatic. It happens quietly. It happens in small decisions. In daily adjustments. In choosing curiosity over shame.

The Reframe - What Was True All Along

I am still learning emotional intelligence.

Still learning rest.

Still learning trust.

Still learning what success means for a life like mine.

I don't know what my legacy will be.

I don't know who will remember me or what story they will tell.

But I do know this: If someone reads these pages and feels less alone, that is enough.

Because the truth is simple. I am not finished.

And neither are you. We are still becoming.

The Reframe Reflection

(What was true all along)

What question could replace "What's wrong with me?" in your life?

What does success look like if you define it for yourself?

Where might you be in a process of becoming rather than failing?

What systems or supports help you function best?

How might your life change if you treated yourself with curiosity instead of judgment?

Afterword

Closing

Not ending. Shifting Directions.

"How silly of me to forget how far I've come, just because I still have far to go"

~Winnie the Poo.

Still Becoming

I am no longer rushing. I used to chase clarity. Now I let it approach me.

I am allowed to change my mind. Past decisions don't trap me. They inform me.

I am not a brand. I am not my output. Not my productivity. Not my résumé of attempts. I exist without justification. I am just human.

I am learning to rest without earning it. Rest is not a reward. It is maintenance.

I am letting go of the scorecard. No more tallying failures against wins. Life doesn't keep books that way.

I am making peace with enough. Enough effort. Enough contribution. Enough presence. More is not always better.

Still Becoming

I am paying attention now.

To what steadies me.

To what drains me.

To what quietly feels true.

And this is what I know:

I am not behind.

I am not broken.

I am still becoming.

Still Becoming

I am not late.

My timeline isn't linear.

Neither is yours.

And today...

I am here.

Breathing. Thinking. Being.

For now, that is enough.

And if you are reading this, you are becoming.

Quote Acknowledgement

Several quotations appear throughout this book to highlight timeless ideas about identity, growth, and the process of becoming. The author gratefully acknowledges the thinkers whose words have contributed to the broader conversation about human development.

The following individuals are quoted within this work: Benjamin Franklin, "What I am to be, I am now becoming." Debbie Fields, "Being good enough never is." Euripides, "Question everything. Learn something. Answer nothing." Charles Darwin, "It is not the strongest of the species that survives, nor the most intelligent, but the one most responsive to change." Janet Fitch, "The phoenix must burn to emerge." David Richo, "Our wounds are often the openings into the best and most beautiful part of us." Michelle Obama, "At fifty-four, I am still in progress, and I hope that I always will be." Winnie the Poo, "How silly of me to forget how far I've come, just because I still have far to go."

These quotations are used to provide historical perspective and thematic reflection throughout the text. Where possible, quotations are attributed to their original authors and appear in brief excerpted form.

The author respects the intellectual contributions of these individuals and acknowledges their influence on the broader dialogue about personal growth, adaptation, and the evolving nature of identity.

All quoted material remains the intellectual property of the original authors or their estates.

Disclamer

This book is distributed with the understanding that the author is not providing professional guidance under any domain of psychological counseling services. The author has made a sincere effort to compose this book, but assurance regarding the content cannot be guaranteed, and any implied Warrant of Merchantability is overtly denied. The advice and tactics discussed herein are recommendations and may not be appropriate for all. It is best practice to seek professional consultation when necessary. The author accepts no liability for any loss of profit or other damage encompassing collateral, specific, individual, subsequent, or other relevant costs.

In reading this information, the reader agrees that under no conditions should the author be accountable for any direct or indirect costs/losses sustained in correlation with reading and using the data contained within this book, including, but not limited to, errors, omissions, or inaccuracies.

www.GretchenLain.com

PRINTED IN THE UNITED STATES OF AMERICA.

www.ingramcontent.com/pod-product-compliance
Lightning Source LLC
LaVergne TN
LVHW010905110826
845149LV00005B/1470
* 9 7 8 1 9 7 2 0 2 4 0 5 8 *